Harry's Hiccups

by Valerie Thomas
illustrated by John Yahyeh

Harcourt Achieve

Rigby • Saxon • Steck-Vaughn

www.HarcourtAchieve.com
1.800.531.5015

Characters

Harry

Miss Ranjan

Contents

3

Chapter 1

Harry's Problem

Harry had the hiccups.

"Hic," he said while he was drinking his orange juice.

Harry's mouthful of orange juice splashed the baby.

The baby thought it was funny.

His mother didn't think it was funny.

"Don't be silly, Harry," his mother said.

"Hold your breath for a minute. Your hiccups will go away."

Harry held his breath for a minute.

His hiccups didn't go away.

Harry still had the hiccups when he got to school.

He tried to hiccup softly in assembly.

"I'm waiting for everybody to be quiet," said Mr. Taylor, the principal.

Everybody was very quiet.

"Hic!" said Harry.

Everybody laughed.

Except Mr. Taylor.

"Who was that?" asked Mr. Taylor.

"Hic!" said Harry again.

Everybody laughed again.

Except Mr. Taylor.

He told Harry to go and sit outside his office.

"Hic," said Harry sadly.

Chapter 2

The Promise

"Why are you sitting here?" asked Miss Ranjan.

She worked in the office.

She was very nice.

"Hic," said Harry. "Hic, hic, hic."

"Have you got the hiccups?" asked
Miss Ranjan.

Harry thought about saying no.

"Yes, hic," he said. "I can't, hic, stop."

"I know how to stop them," said
Miss Ranjan.

"My grandmother told me. But it's
a family secret. I really shouldn't
tell you."

"Please, hic, Miss Ranjan, tell me, hic," said Harry.

"I really need to know."

"Do you promise not to tell anybody else?" asked Miss Ranjan.

"I, hic, promise," said Harry.

Now before you read any more of this story, you have to promise not to tell anybody else.

Miss Ranjan doesn't want everybody to know her family secret.

Do you promise?

OK!

Chapter 3

Miss Ranjan's Family Secret

"Come with me," said Miss Ranjan. She walked out into the school garden.

Harry followed her.

"Hic," Harry said. "What do I, hic, have to do?"

Miss Ranjan was looking under some leaves.

"You have to crunch on a nice fat snail,"
Miss Ranjan said.

"Here's one. It's just the right size."

Miss Ranjan picked up a big fat snail and held it out to Harry.

"Here you are," she said. "Make sure you crunch it up. It works every time."

Harry couldn't believe it! Miss Ranjan wanted him to eat it.

His face turned green. His eyes popped.

Harry felt ill. He thought he was going to be sick.

His stomach turned upside down.

Yuck! Disgusting! Yuck!

"No way!" Harry said.

"I'm not crunching on any snail. I'd rather have hiccups for the rest of my life!"

27

Miss Ranjan looked at Harry.

"Do you still have the hiccups?" she asked.

Harry waited for the next hiccup. He waited and waited.

No hiccups.

Miss Ranjan put the snail back.

"It always works," she said.

Glossary

assembly
a group meeting

crunch
bite or chew food loudly

office
a place where people work

popped
stood out

promise
an agreement to
do something

secret
something you can't
tell other people

splashed
got wet

stomach turned
felt sick in
the stomach

Valerie Thomas

When I was about Harry's age, I would get the giggles and then the hiccups. I couldn't stop the giggles or the hiccups until my sister would scare me. "There's a hairy spider on your leg," she would shout. Or, she would jump out at me from behind a door. A good scare always worked, just like it worked for Harry.

John Yahyeh